BALLOON PUBLISHING

Copyright 2017 Balloon Publishing

No part of this book may be reproduced or trasmitted in any form or by any means except for your own personal use or for a book review, without the written permission from the author

1 - light blue   2 - blue   3 - dark blue   4 - green   5 - dark green
6 - beige   7 - yellow   8 - red   9 - brown   10 - black

1 - brown   2 - green   3 - light blue   4 - dark green   5 - yellow
6 - beige   7 - orange   8 - black   9 - red

1 - dark blue   2 - orange   3 - yellow   4 - pink
5 - light blue   6 - green   7 - red   8 - beige

1 - white   2 - light blue   3 - blue   4 - dark blue
5 - yellow   6 - red   7 - brown   8 - green

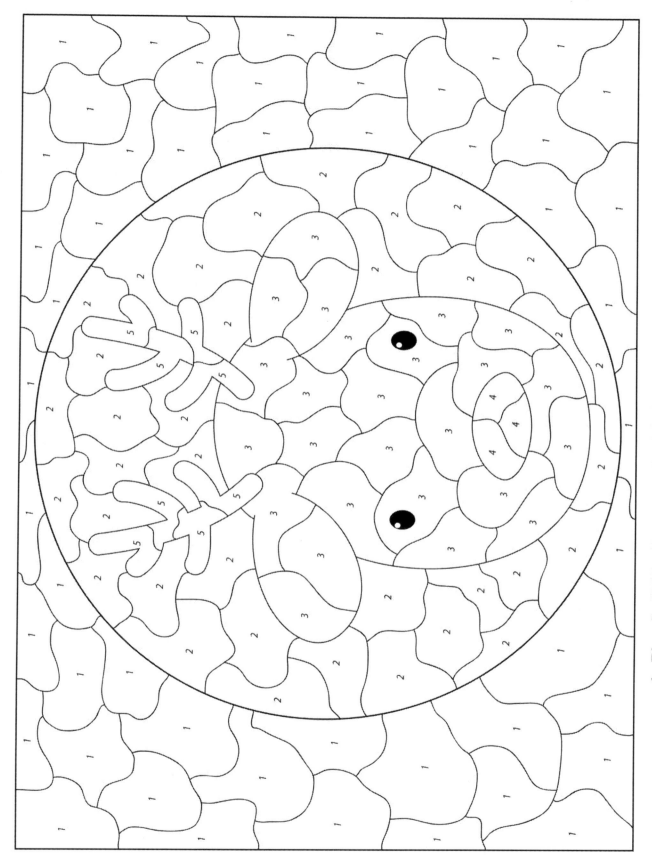

1-Blue 2-White 3-Brown 4-Light Brown 5-Cream

1 - white   2 - light blue   3 - blue   4 - pink   5 - beige   6 - red

1 - light blue   2 - dark green   3 - green   4 - yellow
5 - orange   6 - beige   7 - brown   8 - red

1 - blue   2 - light blue   3 - dark green   4 - green
5 - yellow   6 - brown   7 - red   8 - black

1 - pink 2 - blue 3 - light blue 4 - dark green 5 - green
6 - yellow 7 - orange 8 - beige 9 - brown 10 - red 11 - gray

1 - pink 2 - purple 3 - light blue 4 - yellow
5 - beige 6 - brown 7 - red

1 - blue   2 - light blue   3 - green   4 - yellow
5 - orange   6 - brown   7 - red   8 - gray

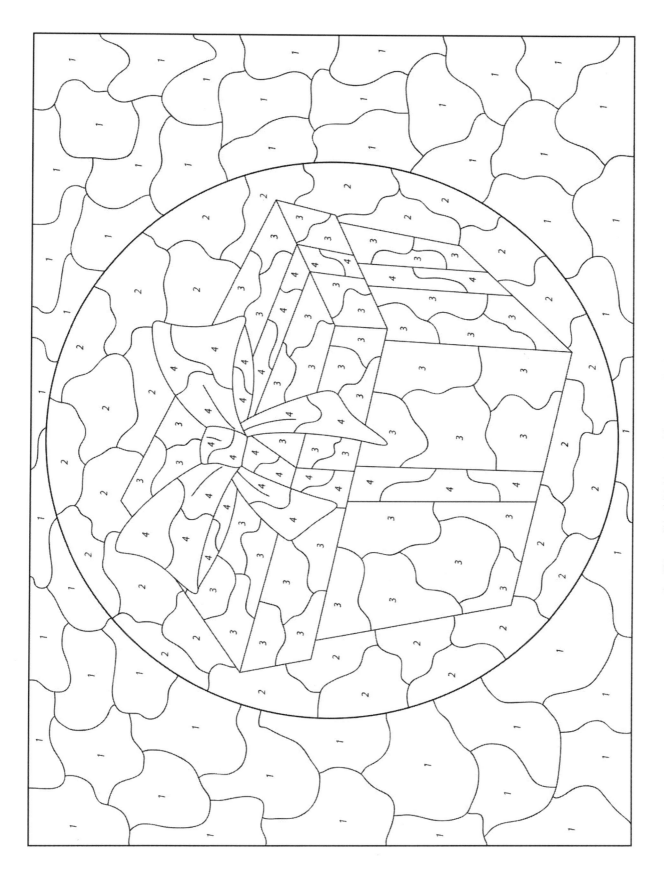

1-Blue 2-White 3-Red 4-Yellow

1 - pink   2 - blue   3 - light blue   4 - dark green   5 - green   6 - yellow
7 - orange   8 - beige   9 - brown   10 - red   11 - dark red   12 - black

1-Light Brown 2-Yellpw 3-Orange 4-Purple 5-Green 6-Red 7-Dark Green 8-light Purple

1 - light blue   2 - blue   3 - green
4 - yellow   5 - orange   6 - dark green

1 - pink   2 - yellow   3 - brown   4 - green

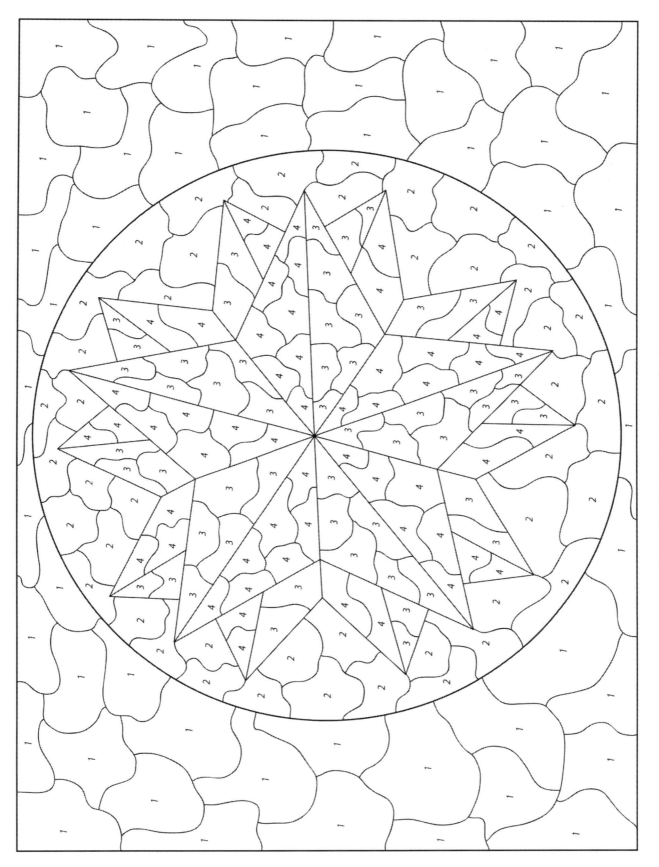

1-Blue 2-White 3-Yellow 4-Orange

1 - white   2 - light blue   3 - gray   4 - green
5 - yellow   6 - orange   7 - brown   8 - dark green

1 - light blue   2 - blue   3 - green   4 - dark green
5 - yellow   6 - gray   7 - black   8 - brown

1 - yellow   2 - brown   3 - green   4 - dark green

1 - green   2 - red   3 - dark red   4 - brown
5 - yellow   6 - black   7 - orange   8 - blue   9 - beige

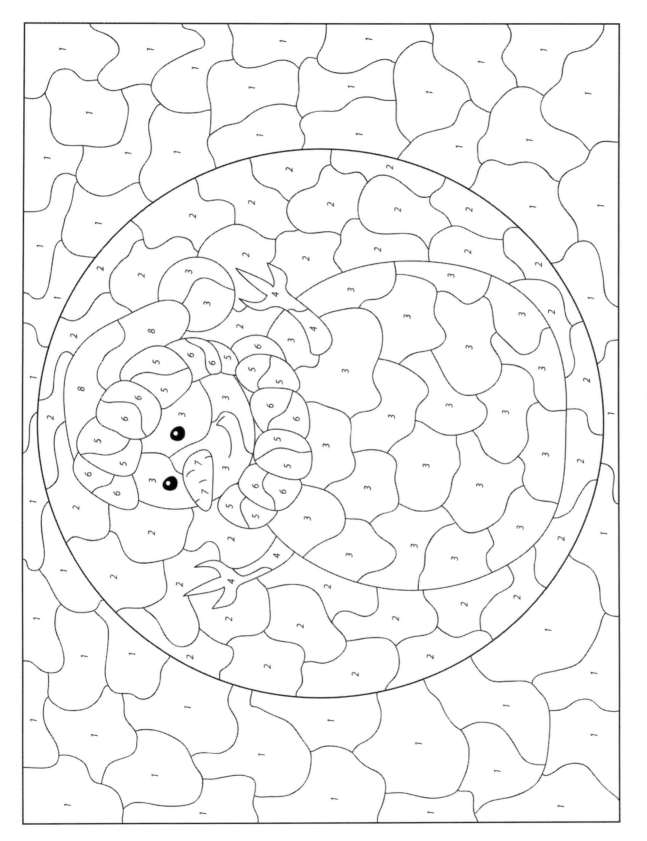

1- Green 2- White 3- light blue 4-Brown 5-Yellow 6-light purple 7- red 8-purple

1 - green   2 - dark green   3 - blue   4 - light blue   5 - beige
6 - yellow   7 - red   8 - orange   9 - brown

1 - light blue   2 - blue   3 - black   4 - dark blue
5 - yellow   6 - orange   7 - pink   8 - red

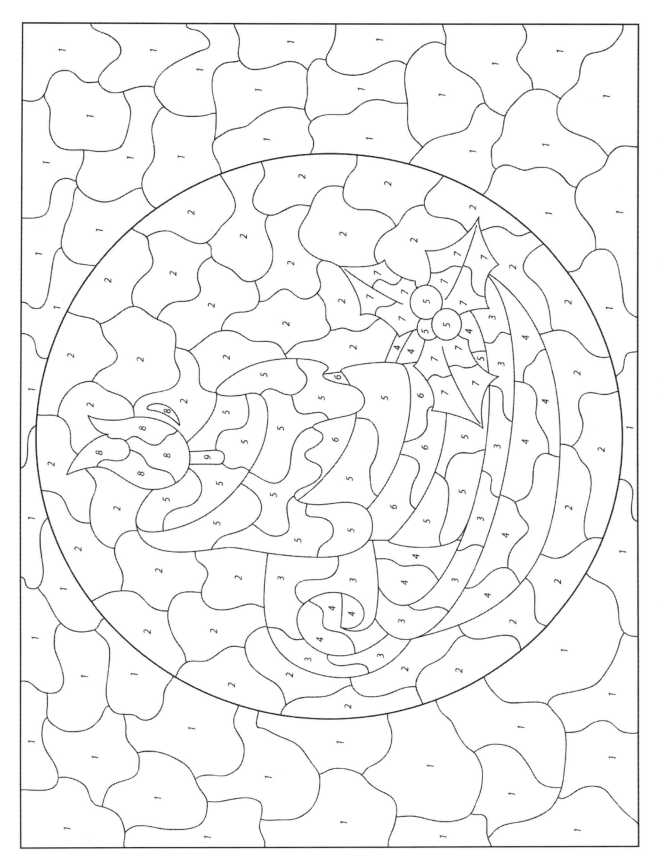

1–Purple 2–Beige 3–Light Brown 4–Brown 5–Red 6–White 7–Green 8–Yellow 9–Black

1 - white   2 - light blue   3 - green   4 - dark green
5 - yellow   6 - brown   7 - red   8 - dark red

Made in the USA
Lexington, KY
26 November 2018